Foreword

If you like clowning around and doing magic tricks, then look no further! In here you'll find great ideas for amazing magic tricks, balloon art and juggling to stun your family and friends. Detailed step-by-step instructions show you how to create fun, funky models from just a few balloons. You'll also learn how to juggle with one, two or three balls, bean bags – or bananas! There are plenty of magic tricks to learn from the Coin Through Hand trick that needs no preparation to the Time-bomb Escape, which is as much fun to set up as it is to perform. You'll also get to know lots of hot tips on how to lay on a really good show with plenty of razzmatazz. So put on your performer's biggest smile and get ready to take the stage!

Contents

A Magic Show 7

Introduction 8

Materials, Tips and Magic
Words 9–13

Projects 14–37

Clowning Around 39

Introduction 40

Materials 41

Basic Techniques 42–43

How to Make Balloon Balls 44

How to Make Bean Bags 45

Projects 46–67

Sneaky, Cheeky Tricks 69

Introduction 70

Materials 72

Equipment 73

Projects 74–93

Index 94

Acknowledgements 96

A Magic Show

Hugh Nightingale

Introduction

So, you want to be a magician? Good! Because magic is fun. Actually, it is *great* fun. Making the tricks is fun, doing the tricks is fun and, most of all, entertaining people with magic is fun.

Some people, and books, say magic is very hard to do because it needs hour after hour, year after year, of never-ending practice. Well, in this chapter you will find lots of tricks that you will be able to do easily with only a little practice. And once you've learnt how to do all the projects shown here, you might go on to learn the more complicated secrets of magic.

Making Things For Your Magic

The Wand

In order to practise magic, you need a few essential props. The most important of these is your wand. You can make one yourself. All you need is a 30 cm length of round wood, called dowel, some masking tape and black and white poster paints. Wrap masking tape around each end of the dowel and paint the wood in-between black. When the paint is dry, remove the tape and paint the ends white. Hey presto! The stick has magically become a wand, ready for you to do some brilliant tricks with.

The Magic Box

An essential prop is a beautifully coloured magic box. This box means you will be able to produce many things you need for your show, out of a box that seems to be empty!

1 First tape over the sharp edges of an empty 850 g baked bean tin. Then glue a rectangle of red card together at the edges, to make a tube wider and taller than the tin. For the outer box, join four identical pieces of stiff card together with masking tape. Ask a grown-up to help you cut out some holes in one piece for the front of the box.

2 Here Lucy has decorated the box to look like an old-fashioned radio. Now paint half of the bean tin and the inside of the box with black poster paint. When the paint is dry, fill the tin with magical things.

3 Put the bean tin, filled with silk handkerchiefs, cards, a small pink rabbit and a plastic fried egg, inside the box. Can you see it? No? That is because you place it in the box with its black side facing the holes in the front, so when you lift out the red tube the box appears empty. After putting the red tube back over the bean tin, you can lift up the radio box, because it has no bottom, to show that it is empty as well.

4 This "illusion" means that Lucy can produce the hankies, cards and rabbit from an "empty" box. She can turn the tin around when it is inside the tube and lift it out, with the egg, to add a funny finish to her trick. Now, once she has put the tin and egg away, she can again show her audience that the tube and box are both empty.

This time, as there is nothing left to hide, she can hold the tube and box up together.

The Hat

Every self-respecting magician has a top hat, and it is needed for many of the tricks in this book.

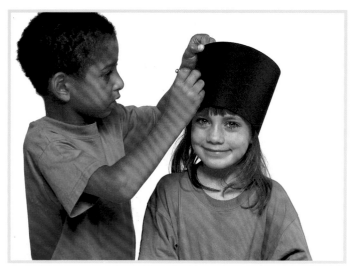

1 Ask a friend to measure around your head. Add 2 cm to the figure and cut a piece of stiff black paper to this length, and about 15 cm wide. Roll the paper into a tube and glue the edges together.

2 For the top of the hat, place the tube upright on a sheet of black paper and draw round it with a white crayon. Draw a second circle about 1 cm wider around the first circle and cut out the outer line. Cut small "V"s around the whole shape between the outer and inner circles. Glue the tabs downwards inside the top of the tube. To make the brim, draw round the shape of your hat onto more black paper. Draw a second circle 1 cm smaller than your tube and a third circle 5 cm larger. Cut out along these last two lines. Cut tabs again and glue them into the bottom of your hat.

3 A secret flap fixed inside your magician's top hat is perfect for hiding things. Cut out a round piece of stiff black paper to fit snugly down into the hat. Tape a flap onto the middle of it with masking tape. Paint the tape black and cut the flap into a semicircle so that it can be held against either side of the hat, with your fingers. If you briefly tip the opening of the hat towards the audience, anything hidden behind the flap will not be seen. They will just see blackness inside the hat and assume the hat is empty.

4 Add some ribbon to the hat to finish it off. Measure round the tube of your hat, and add 1 cm to this. Glue the ribbon round the hat just above the brim with a 1 cm overlap. A black or coloured bow tie will make you really look like a magician.

Performing

Performing magic is all about acting the part of the magician convincingly. When you are doing a trick you must try to believe that magic is really happening. If you believe it, so will your audience.

What to Say

What you say to your audience during your show is called your "patter". The most important thing is to be natural. Talk in your own way. Make up a story to go with the trick and add a few jokes if you would like to get a laugh.

Repeating Tricks

When you have done a good trick, people will ask to see it again. Don't be tempted to repeat it! Your audience might discover the secret of the trick the second time round.

Misdirection

This is the art of making your audience look where *you* want them to look. The audience will look where your eyes are looking or at your moving hands. If you are hiding a coin in your hand, don't look at that hand. Also, never say that a box or hat is "empty" or the audience will be suspicious. Quickly show them the inside and they will assume that it is empty.

Secrets

Always keep your magic secrets to yourself. Store your magic things out of sight, in a case or a closed box.

Appearance

Look smart and especially have clean hands and fingernails. Smile. Look happy. If you feel a little shy in front of an audience, try your tricks out in private first, and even in front of a mirror.

Mistakes

Sometimes things will go wrong (even the most famous magicians sometimes make mistakes!). Don't panic. If you can, correct things and carry on. If you can't, just smile and get the audience involved in another trick. Remember that your audience is there because they want to be entertained and they want you to do well. Practising your tricks in front of a mirror will help prevent the mistakes from happening.

Magic Secrets

Part of the skill of being a magician is keeping things to yourself. In order to show how to do things, we have taken photographs, but whenever you see the top hat symbol, this is a view that the audience should not see.

How Many Tricks?

Don't make your show too long. That way you will leave your audience wanting more and they will ask you for another show on another day. Plan a short show that has a beginning, a middle and an end. And don't forget – smile!

Magic Words

In magic there are many special words. Here are some useful ones for you to learn.

EFFECT   What the audience sees.

GAG   A joke or a funny story.

GIMMICK OR FAKE   A secret part of the prop that the audience does not see.

ILLUSION   When something *seems* to happen but doesn't.

LOAD   The things held in a secret compartment.

PALMING   Keeping something hidden in your hand.

PATTER   Your talk that goes with the trick.

PRODUCTION   Making something appear from nowhere.

PROPS   The things you use for your tricks.

ROUTINE   A series of tricks or moves.

SHUFFLE   To mix up cards in your hands.

SILKS   Silk handkerchiefs.

SLEEVING   Hiding something up your sleeve to make it vanish or ready to appear in your hand later.

SLEIGHT OF HAND   A clever movement of your hand to make magic.

Silk hankies

Coins

Silk scarves

Plastic cups

Cord

Beads

Coloured ribbon

Finger rings

Pack of cards

STEAL To move something from its place secretly.
SWITCH To change one thing for another secretly.
TALK The sound that hidden objects might make – for example, rattle, click, etc.
TRANSPOSITION When something magically disappears from one place to reappear in another.
VANISH To make an object seem to disappear.

Materials

The materials that you will need are always listed. Gather them all together before you start. Work on a suitable surface. Wear an apron if you are painting or gluing, and tidy everything away afterwards. Allow time for paint and glue to dry before moving on to the next stage. Keep a collection of empty cartons, tubes and boxes, etc. Once they have been painted and decorated they are great for magic. Take great care when using scissors or other sharp instruments, and always ask a grown-up to help if you need to use a craft knife.

Black is a very useful colour in magic because a black object in black surroundings becomes almost invisible. So, if the instructions for a trick say to use black, then *do* use black. Finally, take your time and study the photographs and the text carefully. If a photograph shows someone doing a trick with their right hand and you prefer to use your left, don't worry. Just swap things over and do it your own way.

Chocolate money

'Joke' fried egg

Large envelopes

Rubber bands

Soft rope

Paper napkins

Wooden dowel

Decorative stickers

The Dirty Napkin Trick

Magic can have the most powerful effect when people are not expecting it. Here's a trick you could do during a meal. Sarah has this trick well under control. When the person opposite her has sat down and spread his paper napkin on his knee, she asks him for the napkin. She gives the excuse that she has noticed some tiny stains on it. To do the trick she tears off pieces from the centre of the napkin, explaining each time that, "this one's gravy, this one's ketchup", and so on. Finally she opens the napkin out to show that it is whole – without any bits torn out of it. This trick is a real reputation maker. Try it yourself.

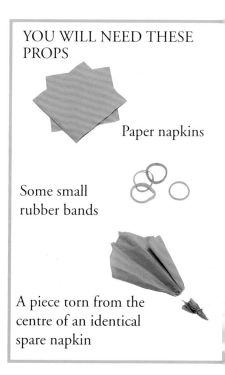

YOU WILL NEED THESE PROPS

Paper napkins

Some small rubber bands

A piece torn from the centre of an identical spare napkin

Tip

Don't use your own napkin for the secret torn piece, as someone might ask to see it afterwards. When you tear off the pieces, remove the rubber band with one of them (see step 6).

14

1 Secretly, under the table, attach the torn piece of napkin to the inside of your left thumb with the rubber band, so that it is hidden in your hand.

2 Borrow a napkin from another diner. No one will notice the torn piece as you reach across the table to take the napkin.

3 Spread the napkin over your left hand and point to the "stains" as you push the centre of the napkin into your hand.

4 The real centre, and the torn centre, are side by side. Here we can see under Sarah's napkin, but don't let anyone else see what is happening.

5 Take both the centres into your right hand. Turn them upside down and put them back into your left hand. Pull up only the torn piece.

6 Tear off pieces, saying they are stained, and put them in your pocket. Remove the rubber band with one of the pieces.

7 Really, you are tearing pieces from the extra piece in your hand. It will look as if you are tearing them from the centre of the napkin.

8 When it looks like you have thoroughly spoilt the napkin, calmly open out the real napkin to the amazement of everyone at the table.

Money from Nowhere!

Tip
For your special coin, to save it melting, carefully take the chocolate out of the foil and make it vanish, in your mouth! Replace it with a disc of cardboard and you can use the coin over and over again.

How about this for a trick? You are holding your empty top hat in one hand, then, with the other hand, you reach up and pluck a gold coin out of the air and drop it into your hat. Then you find another in the air, then another and another. Aribibia is finding coins all over the place, even behind people's ears! Finally he tips his hat onto the table and out pours a shower of golden coins. There are enough coins to hand out to friends after the show. When you do this trick, you will use a specially prepared coin, so make sure you do not give it away but keep it safely for next time.

YOU WILL NEED THESE PROPS

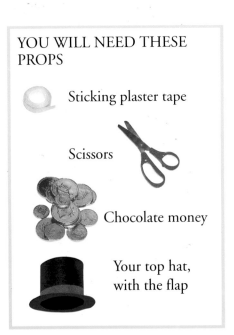

Sticking plaster tape

Scissors

Chocolate money

Your top hat, with the flap

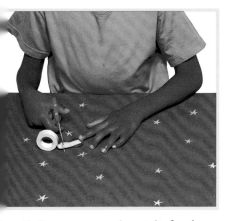

1 Before you start the trick, fix about 4 cm of sticking plaster to one side of your special coin, leaving about 2 cm hanging free.

2 Load one side of your hat flap with chocolate money. With the flap over the money, you can show your audience that the hat is "empty".

3 Hold the coin between your finger and thumb with the plaster stuck to your second and third fingers. Keep the back of your hand to the audience.

4 Hold your hand over the hat, and let the coin go. It will fall behind your fingers, but the audience will believe it has fallen into the hat.

5 Flick the coin up again, and catch it with your thumb. You've caught a coin from the air! Drop it into the hat. Repeat this action several times.

6 Shake the hat to rattle the coins that are already in it. The audience will be convinced that you have caught a hatful of coins from thin air.

7 Finally pour the coins onto the table to show just how many you have collected from thin air.

Magic Wands

It always looks good, in your show, to wave your wand whenever you wish the "magic" to happen. Nhat Han has also discovered some tricks that use the wand itself. She can make the wand "magnetic"; it will cling to her hand with, apparently, nothing holding it in place. She can, or so it appears, push the wand right into her leg and it doesn't hurt her. She can also make her wand stiff one minute and bendy the next. How does she do that?

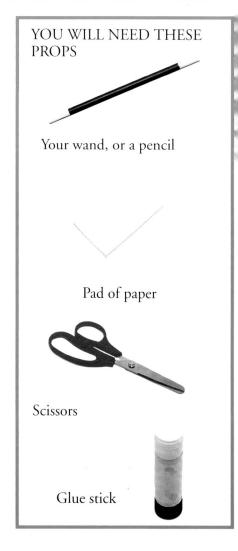

YOU WILL NEED THESE PROPS

Your wand, or a pencil

Pad of paper

Scissors

Glue stick

Magnetic Wand

1 If you are holding a wand and you open your hand, it falls to the floor. Oh, dear!

2 But if you are a magician, like Nhat Han, it will stay in your hand all by itself.

3 Look on the other side of her hand. Can you see her secret? Try it yourself.

Painless Wand

1 Nhat Han rolls up a piece of white paper and glues it to make a tube the same size as the tip of her wand.

2 Nhat Han has pushed the wand right into her leg! But it did not seem to hurt! How did she do that?

3 She hid the lower wand tip in her hand and pushed the paper tube down the wand with her other hand.

Wobbly Wand

1 Nhat Han is trying to bend her wand. It is definitely stiff.

2 Next, she holds it loosely between finger and thumb, about one third of the way down. When she moves it from side to side, it looks wobbly.

The Coin Fold

Tricks with money always get the audience's attention, especially if you make the money disappear and it belongs to someone in the audience! Alexander finds that the coin fold shown here is a very useful method for helping to make a coin vanish easily. But he had to practise hard to perfect his technique, especially making the coin reappear from Michelle's ear.

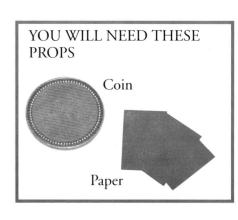

YOU WILL NEED THESE PROPS

Coin

Paper

Tip
Because the audience sees you wrap the coin in the paper, their eyes stay on the paper packet. This "misdirection" allows you to drop the coin into your hand.

1 Place the coin in the middle of the paper and fold about one-third of the paper over it.

2 Press this down. It helps if you leave a coin-shaped impression in the paper.

3 Turn the paper and coin over, carefully, holding the coin in the fold of the paper, as Alexander is doing here.

4 Fold over about one-third from one side.

5 Then fold over about the same from the other side, so that the folds overlap.

6 Now fold the flap at the top over the other folds. Put the package in your left hand and hold a corner of the flap with your left thumb.

7 Gently lift the package, so that the coin slides out of the secret gap and stays hidden in your hand. Hold it with your second and third fingers.

8 Now you can tear up the package in front of the audience. Or you can hand it to a friend to hold, and pretend to find the coin in her ear.

Cutting Coins

Here is a routine that uses the coin fold principle demonstrated in the previous trick, some misdirection and a technique called "sleeving" the coin. The trick is a bit complicated to do, and might need a lot of practice. But if you can do this trick successfully, everyone will be convinced that you really *are* a magician. You will need to wear a jacket, blazer or similar clothing, with an inside breast pocket. Look at the pictures carefully. Notice in particular how Lucy uses her eyes to draw the audience's attention to exactly where she wants them to look, while she is doing the secret move somewhere else.

Tip

Put the scissors in your breast pocket before you start the routine. Place them point down. If you borrow the coin, you could get the lender to sign it with a felt-tipped pen, or remember the date on the coin. This will prove that you are using only one coin.

All the time you are performing the trick, keep your eyes on the packet to misdirect your audience.

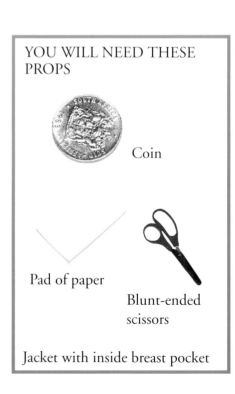

YOU WILL NEED THESE PROPS

Coin

Pad of paper

Blunt-ended scissors

Jacket with inside breast pocket

1 Borrow a coin and do the coin fold as described in Steps 1 to 7 in the previous trick. Keep the coin hidden in your right hand.

2 Reach into your breast pocket for the scissors, but first drop the coin into your sleeve. Keep your arm bent up, so the coin stays near the elbow.

3 Bring out the scissors and cut the packet into little pieces. The coin has vanished! (You know it is in your sleeve by your elbow.)

4 Make up another little packet, keeping your arm with the coin bent. The audience can see that your hands, and the paper, are empty.

5 Rattle the packet and listen to it. Look as if you can hear a coin in there. This misdirects the audience while you drop your left hand naturally to your side. Catch the coin with your fingers as it slides out of your sleeve.

6 Keeping the coin hidden, bring both hands together and quickly tear open the paper packet. The coin that was hidden in your fingers seems to come out of the empty packet.

Middle House Mouse

This trick is loosely based on what's probably the oldest magic trick in the world, the "cups and balls", which is over 2000 years old. When Wura performs the trick using fluffy mice, she tells a story about a mouse who only ever wanted to live in a middle house, never at the end of a row.

Tip

You do not have to use mice. Look in the shops for four identical novelty animals that fit in your cups or you could even make your own.

The beakers or cups need to be of flexible plastic, not china or metal.

To make the bases for your animals, draw around a beaker onto the cardboard. Ask a grown-up to cut out the circle so that it is just a little *smaller* than the mouth of the beaker.

Never ever show more than one mouse at one time. The audience must believe that there is only one.

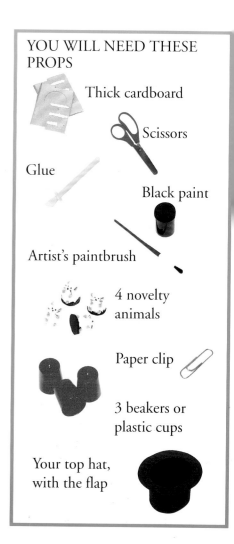

YOU WILL NEED THESE PROPS

Thick cardboard

Scissors

Glue

Black paint

Artist's paintbrush

4 novelty animals

Paper clip

3 beakers or plastic cups

Your top hat, with the flap

1 Ask a grown-up to cut out three circles to just fit inside a beaker. Paint them black. Leave to dry, then glue the circles onto the three mice.

2 Unbend the paper clip to make a hook at each end. Push one end into the fourth mouse. Hook it to your back before starting the trick.

3 Practise lifting up a beaker with a mouse inside. If you squeeze the cup when you lift it, the mouse stays in the cup and seems to "disappear".

4 Now for the performance. Arrange three beakers, each with a mouse hidden inside, in a line. Show the audience only the middle mouse.

5 Squeeze the two end beakers gently as you lift them (to hold the mice inside) to show they are "empty".

6 Swap the two end beakers with the middle one. Then lift the new middle beaker to show that the mouse has magically jumped back.

7 Swap the beakers again. Take the mouse from the end cup, and put it in your top hat. Lift the middle cup. The mouse has "jumped" back again!

8 Repeat until all the mice are in the hat, then show that the hat is also "empty". The audience will see where the mouse is when you turn round!

Postman's Wand

Gerald is demonstrating a really smart trick he has learnt. He puts his wand into an envelope, ready to post it. Then he performs a little magic, and "alakazam", the wand disappears from the envelope and then it reappears in a different envelope on the other side of the room.

Tips

Find some large envelopes that fit your wand, in different colours if possible or decorate them differently.

Make sure the envelopes stay in view at all times. Prop them up against the backs of two chairs if necessary.

Before you put the wand into the envelope, tap the chairs or tables with the wand. This proves that the wand is solid without your actually having to say so, which would seem suspicious.

YOU WILL NEED THESE PROPS

White paper

Glue

Black paint

Artist's paintbrush

Your wand

2 large envelopes

1 Roll up some paper and glue it to make a hollow paper wand. Paint it to look like a real wand. When the paint is dry, slide it over the real wand.

2 Show your audience the two empty envelopes and place them apart on two tables or chairs.

3 Put the wand into one envelope. Shake your head and take it out, secretly letting the real wand slide out of the paper one into the envelope.

4 Put the paper wand into the other envelope, saying, "I prefer it in this one". Now the trick is done, but the audience thinks it has just started.

5 So now it is all acting. Make a magical "swapping over" sign with your arms.

6 The audience saw you put the wand in the second envelope yet you can prove it is now empty by scrunching it up into a ball.

7 With a grand gesture, open up the first envelope to reveal your real wand, which has magically travelled through the air. Magician, take a bow.

Back-flip Card

When people know you do magic, they will often ask to see a card trick. The trouble is, many card tricks involve complicated, finger-twisting moves. But try this: if you can put a pack of cards behind your back, turn the whole pack over and then turn just the top card over, you can do this trick. It is that easy. You have to have a reason for putting the cards behind your back, so explain that anyone can do a card trick when they can see the cards, but it takes a *real* magician to do it behind their back. Here, Michelle tries the trick out on Alexander.

Tip
When someone has chosen a card, ask them to show it to someone else (not you!). This helps to avoid them forgetting which card they chose, which would spoil the trick.

YOU WILL NEED THESE PROPS

Pack of cards

28

1 Shuffle the cards, then hold them like a fan, face-down in your hand. Ask a friend to take a card and remember it, but not to let you see it.

2 While talking about doing tricks behind your back, put the pack behind your back and turn it over. Pick off the top card.

3 Turn this card over and put it back on top of the pack. Do this quite quickly. Then bring the cards to the front again.

4 Hold the cards as a pack. All the cards are face up except the top one. Ask your friend to slide his card into the pack; keep the pack closed.

5 Put the pack behind your back again and pick off the top card.

6 Turn over the top card and put it back on the pack. Then turn the whole pack over while you say you are trying to find your friend's card.

7 Bring the pack to the front again and spread them out. Hocus-pocus! One card is face up, and yes – it is the very card that was chosen!

Coin Through Hand

An impromptu trick is one that you can do anywhere with no preparation or "props". All you need for this impromptu trick is your hands and a coin, which you can borrow. It is also very easy to do and is the first coin trick real magicians usually learn. You can really "act" this one. The audience, at first, think they have caught you out, so they are even more surprised when the coin really does end up in your fist. Michael shows us how to do it.

YOU WILL NEED THESE PROPS

Coin

Tip

Use a medium to large coin, if possible. Small, light coins sometimes stick to your fingers and do not drop when you want them to.

1 Hold the coin above your left fist, as shown, and announce, "I'm going to push this coin through the back of my hand".

2 As you push the coin down, it slides up, out of sight behind your fingers. "There, it's gone through", you can say.

3 Open your fist and say, "Whoops! It must have got stuck, halfway". The audience, though, think they know where it is.

4 "I'll try again", you say as you do the sneaky bit. The sneaky bit is that, as you turn your left hand back over into a fist, your thumb almost brushes against the tips of the fingers holding the coin. Just at this point you let the coin slip out of your fingers, and you catch it in your left hand, which you make into a fist.

5 It all happens so quickly the audience believe it is still hidden behind your fingers, and you say, "I'll give it a harder push this time".

6 Now slowly turn your fist over and open it up. "Ah, there it is!"

Purple Hanky, Red Hanky

Tips
If you choose volunteers who are
wearing the same colours as your silk
handkerchiefs, it is easier for the
audience to follow the trick and for
you to remember where the different
silks are all the time.
    When you tear open the parcel at the
end of the trick, take care not to tear
too deeply or you will expose the
wrong silk.

People in the audience love to come up
and help during a show. For this trick, two
assistants are needed. Nicola cleverly chose
Scott, who was wearing a purple T-shirt, to hold the wrapped purple
silk hanky, and Tope, who was wearing red, to hold the wrapped red
silk hanky. Scott and Tope never let go of their parcels, but Nicola
makes them keep changing sides. A wave of her wand and, "Hey
presto", the hankies have changed places. Now, that *is* magic! How is
it done? Well, the newspapers are not as
ordinary as they seem.

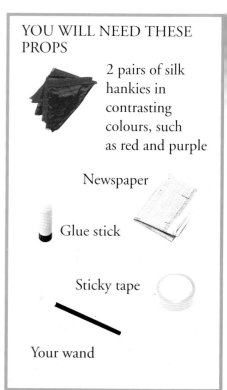

YOU WILL NEED THESE
PROPS

2 pairs of silk
hankies in
contrasting
colours, such
as red and purple

Newspaper

Glue stick

Sticky tape

Your wand

32

1 Before the show, lay out a silk handkerchief on a sheet of newspaper and spread glue round it (not on it!) with the glue stick.

2 Stick a second sheet on top. Do the same with a silk in the other colour. Make a secret mark on the papers, so you know which is which.

3 Fold up the sheets of newspapers and put them on your table, with your wand and the sticky tape. Show the audience the remaining two silks.

4 Wrap the red silk in the paper which has the purple one hidden inside, and make a rough ball shape.

5 Use sticky tape to hold the parcel together. Now wrap the purple silk in the paper with the red one inside, and hold it together with sticky tape.

6 Ask for two volunteers. Give the wrapped red silk to someone wearing red, and the wrapped purple silk to someone in purple.

7 Ask your volunteers to swap places while holding onto their parcels. Wave your wand in the air to make the magic work.

8 Tear open the outer layer of the "purple" parcel. Instead of a purple silk, you pull out a red one! And from the "red" you pull out a purple silk.

X-ray Wand and Ringing Up

Here are two special tricks using magic wands, but with a difference. The second trick uses your wooden wand, but the first one uses a hollow wand. Carl has made a hollow wand by rolling up a sheet of paper and painting it to look like a real one. The X-ray Wand routine is perfect for when you are showing a trick to just one friend, because you actually teach them how to do it. They will be amazed to see a hole right through their hand. Ringing Up is great fun because you can use a ring that you have borrowed from someone in the audience. People always enjoy seeing their own things behaving in strange magical ways.

YOU WILL NEED THESE PROPS

White paper

Glue stick

Black paint

Artist's paintbrush

Black thread

Reusable sticky tac

Safety pin

Your wand

Ring

34

X-ray Wand

1 Roll and glue a sheet of paper to form a tube. Then paint it to look like a wand.

2 Hold the paper wand up to your eye and look through it, keeping both eyes open.

3 Place your other hand, open flat, about halfway along it, beside the wand.

4 Now you will see a hole right through your hand!

Ringing Up

1 Attach a black thread to your wand with sticky tac. Tie the thread to a safety pin; fix this to your waist. Put a ring over the wand to rest on your fist.

2 Wriggle your other fingers as you move the wand slightly away from yourself – the ring starts to rise. How?

3 As you move the wand forwards, the thread attached to the top of your trousers and to the wand moves higher, pushing the ring up the wand.

Time-bomb Escape

How would you like to do a really dangerous and "death-defying" trick to add drama and suspense to your show? Imagine, then, being tied up in a time-bomb and escaping with only seconds to spare. You could pretend to be like Houdini, who was one of the greatest magicians and escapologists of all time. Before you start, ask a grown-up to

make a small hole on each side of the box, about halfway up, for the ropes to go through.

Tips

Decorate your box to make it look really dangerous!

Once you are shut in the box, get the audience to count down from 30 to 1 and then, if you have not escaped, to shout "Bang".

With practice, you will find you can free yourself from the ropes in only a few seconds, but do not jump out too early. The effect is much more dramatic if you leave it until there are only two or three seconds to spare!

YOU WILL NEED THESE PROPS

Large cardboard box that you can fit into

Paints

Artist's paintbrush

Coloured sticky shapes

Long silk scarf

Two lengths of soft rope, each about 3–4 metres long

1 Ask one of your assistants to tie your hands with the scarf. Tie the scarf round one wrist, then the other next to it, firmly, but not *too* tightly.

2 Then ask your assistants to loop a rope over each of your arms. They must hold on firmly to the ends of the ropes, not letting go until the trick is completed. You will be trapped!

3 Climb into the box with an assistant standing guard on each side. Ask them to push the free ends of the ropes out through the small holes in the sides of the box, and then keep hold of them.

4 Squat down inside the box and tell your assistants to close the flaps. Now they can start the countdown with the audience: 30, 29, 28...

5 Even though you are tied up, you will be able to work the rope free. Pull a loop of the rope down the inside of your wrist under the silk scarf.

6 Push the loop back over your hand and let it slide up the back of your wrist. That hand is free. Now do the other one.

7 With only a few seconds of the countdown to spare, jump up like a jack-in-the-box, holding your arms in the air to show they are free.

Clowning Around

Nick Huckleberry Beak

Introduction

So you want to throw things around and catch them again? Create animals out of thin air and rubber? Generally clown around and have fun? Well, you have come to the right place because this is all about juggling and crazy balloon modelling. But be warned – juggling fever is catching and balloon modelling can make your day go with a bang!

Juggling fun

Once you have learned the basics of juggling there is no turning back. You will start with balloon balls and bean bags, then you will want to juggle fruit, plates, cups, sneakers and small pieces of furniture. Before you know it you will be doing Under or Over juggling with the family pet, the Statue of Liberty and an elephant. Nothing is safe – everything can be juggled. Some of the juggling moves are really easy and you will catch on (ha! ha!) in a flash. Other juggling routines will take

This is how all new jugglers look – cross-eyed and confused!

practice, patience and a bit more practice. If you do not have juggling balls, do not worry – there are instructions for making your own balloon balls and bean bags. But if you just cannot wait to get juggling, you can practise with scarves, fruit (ask permission first) or even socks partially filled with uncooked rice. (Cooked rice is impossible to juggle with!) Do not try juggling priceless pieces of crockery or expensive electronic equipment – just yet!

Balloon modelling bug

Twist, twist, bend, bend, stretch, twist and pop! No, this is not a new dance, nor a new breakfast cereal. This is the sound of someone with the balloon modelling bug. The good thing about this bug is that it is fun to pass it on! Without so much as a huff or a puff, you will be able to create a world of hairless dogs, featherless birds and flowers that survive without water. You will even be able to build a light-filled, airy house with nothing more than 17 balloons and a balloon pump.

To start, you will make models for yourself, then you will perform feats of balloon magic at parties, fêtes and carnivals. But once the bug has really taken hold you will be balloon modelling while waiting for the bus, during school and under your duvet at night! It is not that you have gone mad, you have simply become a balloonatic!

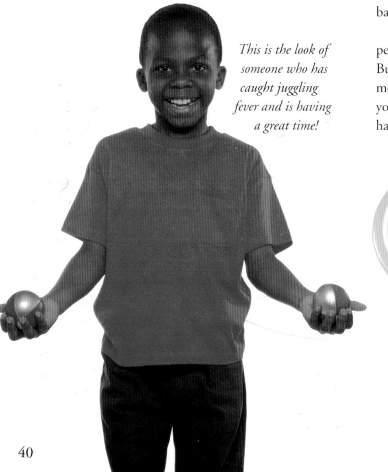

This is the look of someone who has caught juggling fever and is having a great time!

This is a balloonatic. Her balloon modelling skills have gone totally to her head!

Materials

Juggling balls

Bean bags

Juggling rings

Felt-tip pens

Stickers

Scissors

Juggling clubs

Modelling balloons

Balloon pump

You do not need much equipment to be a juggler or balloon modeller. Your greatest assets are your sparkling personality and infectious smile.

Balloon pump There are many types of balloon pumps available, but you must make sure that you get one with a tapered nozzle on the end. These are specially made to inflate modelling balloons. The most effective type of pump is a double-action pump. This pump inflates the balloon when you push the pump in and when you pull it out.

Bean bags These are made from cotton fabric and shaped like pyramids. They are often filled with dried pulses. You can buy them in joke shops and theatrical supply shops, or you can make your own. You will need three or more bean bags.

Felt-tip pens To decorate and draw faces on to your balloon modelling creations you will need indelible felt-tip pens. Indelible means that your drawings will not rub off the smooth surface of the balloon.

Juggling balls These are soft, plastic-covered balls that come in lots of bright colours and patterns. You can buy inexpensive sets of juggling balls in toy shops and joke shops, or make your own using round, party balloons and uncooked rice.

Juggling clubs These can be bought in sets or separately, and they come in various sizes. They are quite expensive. In place of clubs, try your juggling moves with plastic skittles. You can even decorate the skittles to look just like the real thing.

Juggling rings When you become very confident at juggling, you could buy a set of juggling rings. They are made of metal and come in various sizes.

Modelling balloons These are long, thin balloons that come in a variety of colours. You can buy them in bags of 100 in toy and joke shops, and also in specialist theatrical suppliers. All the balloons used in these projects are the '260' type. Modelling balloons can lose some of their quality over time, and are best kept in a cool, dark place.

Scissors You will need a pair of scissors to cut balloons to make balloon balls, to make bean bags and to do one of the tricks.

Stickers You can use stickers to decorate balloon models and juggling equipment. Buy sheets of plain coloured or fancy stickers from toy shops and stationery shops.

Basic Techniques

Inflating modelling balloons and tying knots

Modelling balloons are easier to inflate and less likely to burst if they are warm. You can warm them by stretching them a few times and by keeping them out of the refrigerator. Do not leave balloons in sunlight – this will speed up the process of disintegration.

Bang! Some balloons are (pop! burst!) weaker than others. On average, about one in every 25 to 30 balloons bursts during inflating, so do not (bang!) worry – it is not your fault. Immediately discard the burst balloon and any small pieces that have fallen on the floor by putting them in the dustbin or out of reach of young children and pets.

The only trick to tying a knot in a modelling balloon is patience. If you take it slowly and keep a tight grip on the balloon, the balloon will be tied in knots, not you!

1 **Inflating the balloon** – carefully insert the nozzle of the pump into the mouth of the balloon for about 2cm (³/₄in). Hold the balloon in place. If you let go of the balloon while it is being inflated, you can easily imagine what happens.

2 Start inflating your balloon, but always leave an uninflated bit at the end. This is important as each time you twist the inflated balloon air will be forced down the balloon. The more twists used to create a model, the longer the uninflated end should be.

3 **Tying a knot** – this is often the cause of much frustration, but really it is not difficult. Hold the end of the mouth of the balloon tightly to keep it sealed. Then stretch the neck of the balloon around two fingers, as shown. Do not pull too tightly – it hurts. Ouch!

4 Pull on the end of the balloon until it crosses the neck of the balloon and the two fingers. Hold with the thumb.

5 Tuck the end of the balloon down between the two fingers and through the circle – in other words, tie a knot!

6 Keeping hold of the end, slip your fingers out of the knot and pull it tight. Phew!

Decorating your balloon models

You can make your balloon models more colourful, realistic or comical by drawing on them or decorating them.

The simplest and quickest way to decorate balloons is to use indelible felt-tip pens. As well as using a variety of bright colours, get hold of a white pen if possible. White is really effective when drawing eyes, as it makes them stand out.

Eyes, a nose and mouth are probably the first things you will want to give your animal balloon models. Why not also draw on paws, feathers or fur, or just wild and wonderful patterns? You could give Pampered Pooch, for example, a fancy collar and name tag. If you are making a model for a friend, you could write their name or a message on it. A balloon model elephant that says 'Happy Birthday' on one side would make a very unusual birthday card.

You can also use small stickers to decorate your models. Stickers come in lots of different shapes, textures and colours. There are even sticker packs of eyes, noses, ears and other facial features. Once your sticker is in position, you will not be able to remove it without bursting the balloon.

To apply paint to a balloon model, you first have to mix PVA glue into the paint before you apply it. The PVA glue will make the paint stick to the balloon. Apply the paint gently and use a soft brush.

Juggling safety tips

Do not attempt to juggle with sharp or pointed utensils or heavy objects. Sharp things will cut you, and heavy objects will give you nasty bump on your head or will land slap, bang, ouch on your little toe!

Make sure you have lots of room around you and above you when juggling. Ask an adult to move furniture out of the way so that you do not trip over. Breakable items should be moved to another country for safe keeping!

Just as well this girl was only juggling balloon balls!

Balloon modelling safety tips

Although we set out to have fun with balloons, they can be dangerous, so please follow these few simple precautions. Make sure your friends are also aware of these rules.

❖ Always keep uninflated or burst balloons away from young children and animals to prevent choking accidents.
❖ Never put a whole balloon or a piece of a balloon in your mouth.
❖ Keep balloons away from your eyes, especially when stretching or inflating them.
❖ Always use a balloon pump. Modelling balloons are very difficult to inflate and cause damage to the lungs or ears if you try to inflate them without a pump.
❖ Do not play with balloons in the kitchen – a balloon may land on a hotplate or ignited gas ring – or near open fires or radiators.
❖ Dispose of burst balloons immediately by putting them in a waste bin.

How to Make Balloon Balls

Balloon balls are easy and fun to make. They are also very colourful. To start your juggling career you will need three balloon balls.

1 Cut the stems off two balloons so that you are left with the round part of each balloon. Fill a plastic bag with 1½ cups of rice. Seal in the rice by folding the bag around itself.

2 Insert the bag containing the rice into one of the cut balloons. This is a bit fiddly as you have to be careful not to split the bag or the balloon. Do not worry if part of the plastic bag is still visible.

3 Insert the balloon and bag of rice into the second balloon. Make sure the second balloon covers any visible bits of the plastic bag. It does not matter if a part of the first balloon is still visible.

When stretched over the balloon ball, the holes in the outer balloons allow the colours of the balloons beneath to show through. Do not stop now, you have two more balloon balls to make!

4 Cut the stem off another balloon and cut a few small holes into the round part of the balloon. Stretch this balloon over the balloon ball. Repeat using another cut balloon.

How to Make Bean Bags

Get out your sewing thread and needle, it is time to make a juggler's favourite piece of equipment – bean bags!

YOU WILL NEED THESE MATERIALS

Scissors

Uncooked rice

Sewing needle and thread

Remnants of cotton fabric

10cm (4in) square of card

Small plastic bags

1 Using the square piece of card as a template, cut out two squares of fabric. To make three bean bags you will need six squares of fabric.

2 Place two squares of fabric right sides facing. Thread the sewing needle and tie a knot at the end of the thread. Sew the squares together along three sides. Turn the fabric bag the right way out.

3 Fill the plastic bag with 1 to 2 cups of rice. Seal the plastic bag by wrapping the bag around itself. Place the plastic bag containing the rice inside the fabric bag.

You have now made your first bean bag – only two more to go. Try to use differently patterned or coloured fabric for each one. It will make it easier to follow the movement of each bean bag when you start practising.

4 Fold over the fabric to make a hem around the opening of the fabric bag. Hold the opening so that the two stitched seams touch, as shown, and sew the edges together to make a pyramid.

One-ball Workout

Just like an athlete who has to do warm-up exercises before he or she can take to the track, a juggler also goes through a warm-up workout. These moves will help you to become familiar with the weight and shape of the ball, how it moves through the air and how to anticipate where it will fall. Sounds difficult? Not once you have learned the knack. Do this workout every time before a juggling practice session.

YOU WILL NEED

1 juggling ball, balloon ball
or bean bag

Handy hint

This workout can be done using all sorts of objects – sneakers, tennis balls, oranges or even elephants (only small ones, of course!). A good juggler can juggle anything, so now is the time to get in some funny juggling practice.

1 **Clap in time exercise** – this first exercise is really easy. Hold a ball (or small elephant) in your right hand. See, I told you this was easy.

2 Throw the ball in an arc just a little way above your head. While the ball is in the air, clap your hands. Keep your eye on the ball.

3 Catch the ball in your left hand. Now throw the ball from the left hand to the right hand and clap while the ball is in the air.

4 **Under the leg throw** – hold the ball in the right hand and put it under your raised right knee. Throw the ball up, clap and then catch the ball in your left hand. Repeat with the left hand.

5 **Behind the back throw** – hold the ball behind your back in your right hand. Throw the ball up and over your left shoulder. Catch the ball in your left hand. Repeat with the left hand.

6 **Dizzy spin throw** – this exercise tests your balance. Throw the ball up with your right hand. While it is in the air, spin around once. Then catch the ball in your left hand.

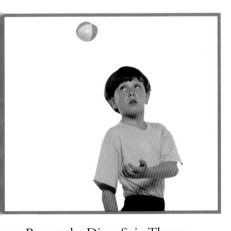

7 Repeat the Dizzy Spin Throw, throwing the ball from your left hand to right hand. Spin in the opposite direction. Are you feeling dizzy yet?

The hard workout

Repeat each One-ball Workout exercise five times with each hand. When you can do each exercise without dropping the ball, it is time to move on to the hard workout!

To do the hard workout, repeat the exercises above, but this time throw the ball a little higher and instead of clapping or spinning once, clap three times or spin around twice.

When you can do the hard workout without dropping the ball, do them with your eyes closed. Just joking !

Two-ball Juggle

Do not panic – two-ball juggling is not as hard as it looks. The secret is to keep your eyes on the balls at all times. Forget about your hands, they are always on the end of your arms. The second part of this exercise is called Juggler's Nightmare. Throwing the balls is easy. The hard part is keeping your hands crossed. Experienced jugglers even find this trick difficult.

Two juggling balls, balloon balls or bean bags

Handy hint

You can make all these exercises harder by clapping or spinning around while the balls are in the air. If you can do Juggler's Nightmare and spin at the same time, it is time you got a job in the circus!

This boy is smiling now, but just you wait till he tries Juggler's Nightmare. When you can do Juggler's Nightmare successfully, challenge your friends to try.

1 Hold a ball in each hand. Throw both balls straight up in the air. Do not throw them too high – just above your head is fine. Catch the balls. Repeat this exercise five times.

2 Stage two of the Two-ball Juggle is to throw the balls so they cross in mid-air and are caught by the opposite hand. Throw one ball a little higher than the other, so they do not collide.

3 For stage three, hold a ball in each hand and throw the balls straight up as in step 1. While the balls are in mid-air, cross over your hands and catch the balls. Try not to go cross-eyed!

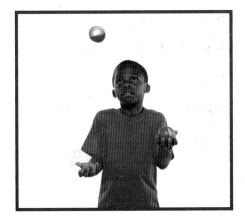

4 If you can do this next exercise, you will be juggling three balls within ten minutes. Hold a ball in each hand and relax – this will not hurt a bit!

5 Throw the right-hand ball in an arc above your head in the direction of the left hand. Just as it starts to fall get ready to throw the left-hand ball.

6 Throw the left-hand ball in an arc toward your right hand. Catch the right-hand ball in your left hand, and the left-hand ball in your right hand.

7 **Juggler's Nightmare** – this move is a nasty twist on the one in step 3. Hold a ball in each hand and cross over your arms, as shown.

8 Throw both balls up at the same time so that they cross over and land in the opposite hand. The trick is you have to keep your hands crossed!

9 Catch both balls. Are your hands still crossed? If so, well done. If not, try again. It can take some time to get the hang of Juggler's Nightmare.

49

Three-ball Frenzy

You had to do it sometime, so grab three juggling balls or bean bags and get ready to perform your first real juggle. You can practise this using scarves if you like. Scarves move more slowly and are easier to catch.

YOU WILL NEED

3 juggling balls, balloon balls or bean bags

Handy hint

Remember to throw the balls straight up, not forwards. If you throw them forwards you will soon be walking all over your audience. You will have enough to do juggling and catching three balls without taking a leisurely stroll at the same time!

This boy has just found out something really important. If he counts 'one, one, one, one' when juggling, it helps him to slow down. Counting 'one, two, three, four' makes you speed up and you know what happens then – all the balls end up on the floor!

1 Hold two balls in your right hand. (If you are left-handed, you may want to hold them in your left hand.) Hold one ball in the other hand.

2 Throw the yellow ball in an arc over your head. Keep your eye on the ball and be ready to throw the turquoise ball when the yellow one starts to fall.

3 At this stage the turquoise ball is in mid-air and you have caught the yellow ball. Throw the red ball when the turquoise ball starts to fall.

4 Catch the turquoise ball but keep your eyes on the red ball that is hurtling over your head. Do not look at your hands when they are catching.

5 You can start to breathe again now for you are about to catch the red ball. Well done – you have successfully completed your first three-ball juggle.

6 **Flashy start** –When you are confident doing steps 1 to 5, try this crowd-pleaser. Hold three balls as in step 1.

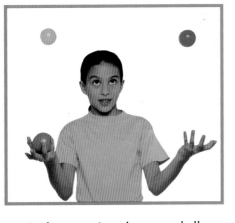

8 Catch the two balls – one in each hand. When the last ball starts to fall, throw the two balls straight up in the again. Catch the last ball in the opposite hand and then start a normal three-ball juggling routine.

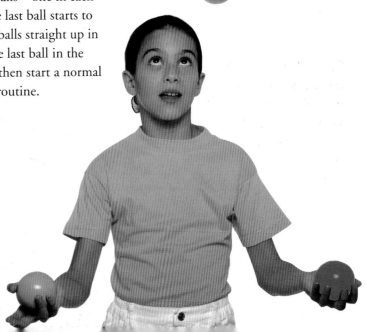

7 At the same time throw one ball from each hand straight up. As the balls start to fall, throw the remaining ball in an arc over your head. Keep your eyes on the balls, not your hands.

Crazy Juggling

This is a juggling trick for those who really like to perform. You will have to deliver your lines convincingly and look totally embarrassed at the result of your silly trick.

6 bean bags

1 Tell your audience that you are going to do an impression of the world's worst juggler. Hold three bean bags in each hand. Then wriggle your body and move your hands about as though you are readying yourself to juggle. Keep looking upward.

3 As soon as the bean bags land – thud, thud, thud – on the floor, make a desperate face and pretend to be upset. You are, after all, the world's worst juggler!

2 The dramatic movement has arrived – throw all six bean bags in the air. Run about waving your arms in the air trying to catch the bags as they fall. Do not catch any bean bags.

Monkey Juggling

No, you are not going to juggle monkeys, only bananas. This trick is as easy as falling out of a tree, but to make it funny you have to get in some silly monkey business.

YOU WILL NEED

3 bananas or bean bags

1 Place a beanbag or banana under each arm and hold one in your left hand. Cup your right hand. Release the bean bag tucked under your right arm and catch it smoothly in your right hand while making monkey noises.

2 While still holding the bean bag in your right hand, tuck the bean bag in your left hand under your right arm. As you bring your left arm down, release the bean bag tucked under your left arm.

3 Catch the bean bag in your cupped left hand. Tuck the bean bag held in your right hand under your left arm. As you bring your right arm down, release the bean bag tucked under your right arm.

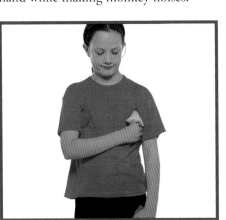

4 Catch the bean bag in your cupped right hand. Now you start the whole routine again. The aim is to practise this so that you become very quick. By the way, did you keep doing the monkey noises or were you just going bananas?

To really get a laugh, start to swing your arms and lope around the stage like a monkey.

53

Under or Over

This time you are going to juggle three balls under your legs and over your shoulders. Whatever next – juggling under water? The important thing with this trick is to raise your leg, rather than bend down. It certainly makes it easier to balance.

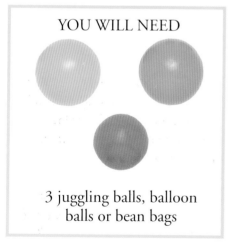

YOU WILL NEED

3 juggling balls, balloon balls or bean bags

Handy hint

If you are left-handed, then hold two balls in your left hand and one in your right. Follow the step-by-step instructions, but use your left hand whenever the right hand is mentioned. Likewise, use your right hand when the left is mentioned in the instructions.

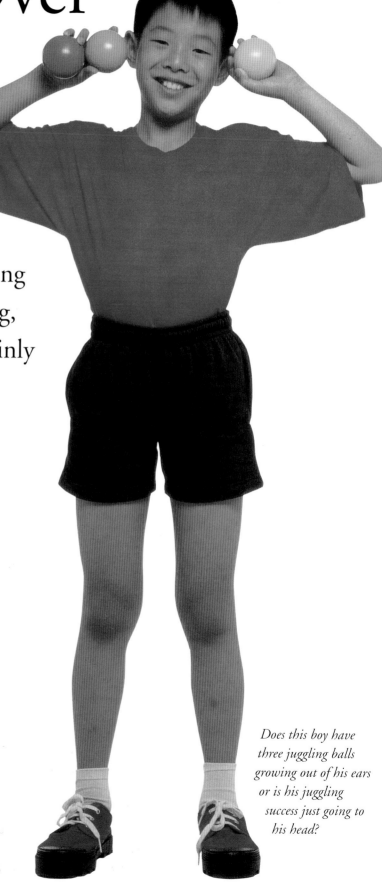

Does this boy have three juggling balls growing out of his ears or is his juggling success just going to his head?

1 **Under the leg juggle** – hold two balls in the right hand and one in the left. Raise your right leg, as shown, and get your balance.

2 Put your right hand under your leg and throw the green ball in an arc toward your left hand. Keep watching the ball.

3 While the green ball is in mid-air, throw the blue ball in your left hand in an arc toward your right hand. Catch the green ball in your left hand.

4 Catch the blue ball in your right hand. Continue juggling normally (see Three-ball Frenzy) except that you will throw the balls from under your leg, not in an arc over your head.

5 **Over the shoulder juggle** – hold two balls in your right hand behind your back. Hold one ball in your left. Look over your shoulder, as shown. Do not stiffen up – try to relax.

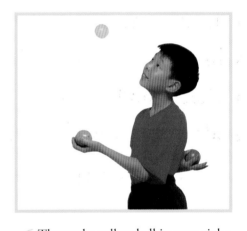

6 Throw the yellow ball in your right hand so that it travels upward and then down over your left shoulder. Move your right hand around to the front of your body.

7 When the yellow ball starts to fall, throw the green ball in your left hand in an arc toward your right hand. Catch the yellow ball in your left hand.

8 Catch the green ball in your right hand. Now you can commence to juggle in the normal way, except that you will throw balls over your shoulder.

When you become really good at Under or Over, you can do it with juggling clubs. But mind that you do not hit yourself on the head!

Pampered Pooch

Here we go with your first balloon model. This one should look like a poodle, but do not worry if your first attempt looks more like a bunch of grapes – keep trying!

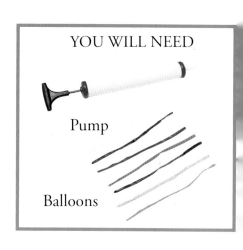

YOU WILL NEED

Pump

Balloons

1 Inflate and knot a balloon, leaving 10cm (4in) uninflated at the end. Starting at the knotted end, twist the balloon to make three 8cm (3in) long bubbles. Hold on to the balloon.

2 To form the ears, twist the second and third bubbles around each other. The bubbles are now locked in place. The first bubble forms Pampered Pooch's head and nose.

3 Make three more bubbles slightly larger than the other bubbles. Twist the second and third bubbles around each other to make the front legs.

To make models of other breeds of dog, like the long-bodied and short-legged dachshund, simply alter the length of the bubbles.

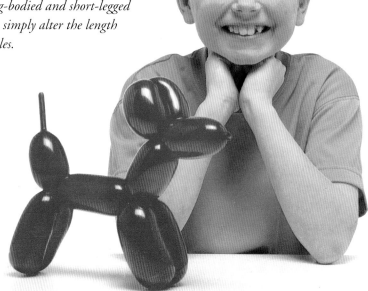

4 Make three bubbles in the other end of the balloon. The first bubble should be 8cm (3in) long, the other two should be slightly larger. Twist together the second and third bubbles to make the hind legs. The bubble nearest the end is pooch's fluffy tail.

Parrot on a Perch

Polly Parrot is a popular bird! When Polly is not on her perch, you can sit her on your head by putting the loop around your chin. No wonder Polly thinks you are crackers!

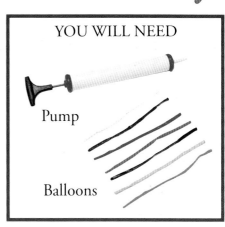

YOU WILL NEED

Pump

Balloons

1 Completely inflate a balloon and knot the end. Make a small bubble at the knotted end of the balloon for the parrot's beak.

2 Pull the knot and bubble down beside the rest of the balloon. Twist and lock the knot around the balloon to form another slightly larger bubble. The first bubble is the beak and the second bubble is Polly's head.

3 You will wonder where the next move is leading, but do not worry, it will soon become obvious. Bend the balloon to form a large loop. Twist the balloon around itself about 18cm (7in) from the end to make the tail.

This parrot on a perch makes a great decoration. Simply tie one end of a piece of string around the top of the perch and attach the other end to your bedroom wall or ceiling.

4 This is the tricky bit, so good luck! Position the tail in the middle of the loop. Pinch and twist the tail and the two sides of the loop together, approximately 8cm (3in) below the head, to make the parrot's body and wings. All you need to do now is arrange Polly on her perch.

Big Elephant

Here is an elephant with a great, long trunk. If you want, you can make the ears bigger and the trunk shorter – it will look just as funny!

1 To make this balloon model, you start with the tail and work up towards the head. Inflate the balloon, leaving 8cm (3in) uninflated at the end. Knot it. Twist the balloon to make three bubbles, the first 2.5cm (1in) long and the next two 4cm (1½in) long.

2 Twist and lock the two larger bubbles together to form the back legs. The smaller bubble is the elephant's tiny tail. Make three more bubbles, each 4cm (1½in) long, for the body and front legs. Hold on to the bubbles until they are locked into position.

3 Twist and lock the end two bubbles to make the front legs. Make two bubbles – one 2.5cm (1in) long and one 11cm (4½in) long – to make the neck and one ear. Twist the long bubble around the small one.

4 Make another 11cm (4½in) bubble. Twist and lock it around the neck bubble. This is the elephant's other ear. Slightly bend the remaining length of balloon to make the enormous, trumpeting trunk.

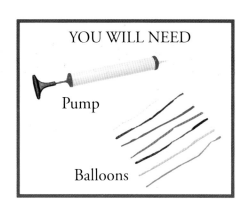

Tiny Mouse

Did you know that elephants are terribly frightened of mice? Funny to think that something so enormous and strong could be scared of something so tiny and cute.

To make a tiny mouse, you only need a tiny balloon, so inflate only the first third of the balloon. This will leave the balloon with a long uninflated tail. Tie a knot in the end.

2 To form the head, twist three small bubbles each 4cm (1½in) long. Twist and lock the second and third bubbles together to make the ears. The first bubble forms the head and nose.

3 Twist three small bubbles of the same size to make the neck and front legs. Twist and lock the second and third bubbles as before. See, balloon modelling is easy!

Make a family of tiny mice using different coloured balloons.

4 Can you guess what comes next? That's right, three more small bubbles! Twist and lock these to form the body and back legs. The rest of the balloon is the mouse's long tail.

King of Hearts

This smart crown will make you look like the King of Hearts. You do not have to add a balloon to the top of your crown, but why not? You could add a heart-shaped or round balloon, or even some bits of ribbon. Go on and make a crown fit for a king – or queen.

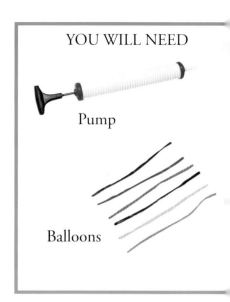

YOU WILL NEED

Pump

Balloons

1 Fully inflate two balloons and knot the ends. Twist the balloons together, as shown, to make a headband. The free ends of both balloons should be the same length.

2 Find the mid-point of the free end of each balloon. Twist the two balloons together at the mid-points.

Why not have a balloon hat-making contest to see which of your friends can create the wackiest hat?

3 Make a small bubble in the end of one free end. Twist it around the headband, halfway along one side.

4 Make a bubble in the other free end. Twist it around the headband, halfway along the opposite side. All loyal subjects should now bow to the king!

Dashing Sword

This Dashing Sword looks great, but it is not much chop at cutting anything. At least you and your friends will not hurt each other during mock battles! Make a scabbard by joining two balloons together and wearing them around your waist.

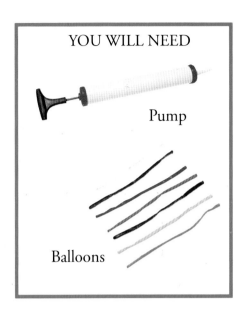

YOU WILL NEED

Pump

Balloons

1 Inflate a balloon, leaving 5cm (2in) uninflated at the end. Knot the end. Push the knot inside the balloon about 4cm (1½in) and hold it in position. Use your other hand to squeeze the balloon round the knot. Twist the balloon to hold the knot in place.

2 Twist the balloon to make two bubbles. The first bubble will form the handle. The second, longer bubble will form one third of the shield that protects the hand. Bend the longer bubble, then twist and lock it around the first bubble.

3 Twist the balloon to make another third of the protective hand shield. Twist and lock it around the handle, as before. If you make the hand shield bubbles too long, your Dashing Sword will be really short!

Balloon swords burst very easily, so make your sword fights really gentle or be ready to make lots of swords.

4 Make the final part of the hand shield in the same way.

Crazy Balloon Tricks

Impress and amuse your family and friends with these brilliant balloon stunts. You must never tell anyone the secrets of how to do the tricks!

You are bound to be asked to repeat these tricks, so have a few balloons prepared.

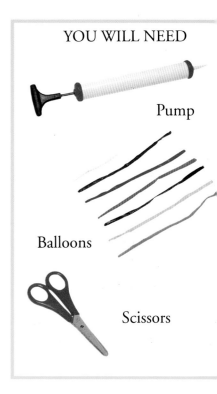

YOU WILL NEED

Pump

Balloons

Scissors

1 **Appearing bubble** – to prepare for this trick, inflate a balloon and leave 18cm (7in) uninflated at the end. Knot the balloon. Grip the uninflated section with both hands, as shown. Now stretch the balloon. Go on, really pull!

2 To perform the trick, show the audience that it is an ordinary balloon. Twist a bubble 5 to 8cm (2 to 3in) long at the end of the balloon and hold it in your hand. The audience should not see you do this.

3 Tell the audience that you will make a bubble appear at the end of the balloon. Without the audience seeing, squeeze the bubble really hard. A small bubble should magically appear at the end of the uninflated section.

4 **Magic balloon** – to prepare, take two uninflated balloons of the same colour and cut the end off one of them with a pair of scissors. Slip the cut-off end on to the end of the whole balloon.

5 Tell your friends you have a magic balloon and offer to show them a trick with it. Inflate the balloon, but leave the end uninflated. There needs to be a space between the real end of the balloon and the false end.

6 Hold the inflated end of the balloon with one hand, and the false end with the other. Say to your friends that the balloon is too long and that you are going to make it shorter. Pull sharply on the false end.

7 Your friends will not understand why the balloon has not deflated.

Practise and prepare

It is important that you practise and prepare these tricks before you perform them in front of an audience. It is also a good idea to work out exactly what you are going to say.

Do not forget that some of the moves in these tricks are not meant to be seen by the audience.

Bunch of Tulips

What a beautiful bunch of tulips! These balloon flowers last longer than real tulips and they do not need watering! You could tie a big, colourful ribbon around the stems to make a lovely present.

1 Inflate only 8cm (3in) of one balloon, leaving a very long uninflated section. This will be the stem of the tulip. Knot the end. Hold the two ends of the inflated section of the balloon, as shown.

2 Use your finger to push the knot into the balloon until the knot reaches the other end of the inflated section. This will take a little bit of practice, so do not give up after the first attempt.

3 Take hold of the knot with the other hand. Remove your finger from inside the balloon. While holding the knot very firmly, twist the balloon several times. This will hold the knot in place.

4 Now that you have made one beautiful tulip, go on to make a whole bunch in different colours.

If you want to be really cunning, you can make the tulip stand up by inserting thin plastic straws inside the balloons before you inflate them.

Sunflowers

Just like real sunflowers, these balloon sunflowers are enormous! But unlike the real ones, they will not turn their colourful heads to face the Sun. Make two or three and use them to decorate your bedroom.

YOU WILL NEED

Pump

Balloons

1 Inflate two balloons, leaving only a very short uninflated end in each one. Knot the ends. Tie the knotted end of each balloon to the other end to form two circles.

2 Now for a bit of fun and a lot of squeaking. Twist each circle to make a figure 8 shape. Both ends of the figure 8 should be the same size.

3 Twist the two figures of 8 together to make a cross. These are the gigantic petals of your sunflower. Let us hope there are no gigantic bees or caterpillars about.

4 Inflate another balloon, once again leaving only a small uninflated end. Twist a loop in the centre of the balloon. Twist another loop next to the first one. These are the leaves and stem.

To finish, insert the end of the stem balloon through the centre of the petals. Twist the stem to lock it in place.

Building a Balloon House

This house is a great favourite and it is really fun to build. Use your imagination to add extra rooms or to make balloon doors, windows, trees, lamp-posts and furniture. Make it as big as you like, but remember that your house will not be very warm in winter and you will get soaked when it rains!

YOU WILL NEED

Pump

At least 17 balloons

This balloon house is multi-coloured, but you could make your house using red balloons for the walls and black balloons for the roof.

1 Inflate 17 balloons and knot the ends. Seventeen balloons is enough to build this one-room house, but for grander designs you will need more balloons. Twist the ends of four balloons together to make a square. Make another square in the same way.

2 Use four more balloons to link the two squares together and make a cube. Twist the ends of the balloons to lock them in position. Is it time for a tea-break yet?

3 Attach a balloon to each top corner of the cube. Twist the end of two balloons together to make a triangle. Do the same with the other two balloons. To finish the roof, link the triangles with a balloon.

Once you have built your first house, go on to create other types of houses. This one is called the Wonky Tepee model!

4 Well done! You have built a home you can truly call your own. Now is the time to work out ways of adding extra rooms or making your house a little more private.

Pop! goes your dream house

Before you start constructing your house make sure that the floor beneath it is smooth and free of splinters or sharp edges. Sadly, your dream house will collapse if the balloons are punctured. It might be a good idea to cover the building site with an old sheet before you start inflating the balloons.

Cheeky,
Sneaky Tricks

Nick Huckleberry Beak

Introduction

To put on a really amazing magic show you need to know the three Ps. No, not three garden peas, but the three magic Ps – preparation, presentation and performance. You can forget all about that abracadabra mumbo-jumbo, just remember the three Ps.

Preparation

To avoid getting halfway through a wickedly good trick and realizing that you are missing a vital piece of equipment, you must be prepared. You must have everything you will need at your fingertips. The only way that you can be properly prepared is to make a list of the items that are required for each trick. As you gather them together, tick them off the list. Simple idea, but it works. Have you made your list yet? No, then get to it!

Presentation

This is all about how you dress and act in front of your audience. Presentation is very important if you want your magic show to be a great success. To find out more about presentation read Magical style.

Performance

You have decided to put on a show. Congratulations! First thing you must do is work out which tricks you will do and the order you will do them in. There are no rules for this, but remember that a short show full of knock-out tricks is better than a long show with only a few good tricks.

This trick is in the bag (or should that be envelope?) because this girl has everything prepared.

The best way to give your magic show atmosphere is to use music. Try to match the speed and mood of the music to the pace and style of your act. If you are doing lots of quick tricks, use fast music. If your show is spooky and full of shocking surprises, find a piece of really creepy music.

If you do not use music then you will have to write a script and rehearse the words you are going to say. You may want to introduce each magic trick or tell a little story about where you learned a certain trick. But whatever you say, it is a good idea to have prepared it. It also never hurts to have a couple of good jokes up your sleeve. These can be used to entertain your audience while you get your next trick ready. Do not use any bad jokes – only I am allowed to use them.

Magical style

Even if you can do some of the hardest magic tricks in the world, your show might flop if your presentation style is dead boring. To be a big hit with an audience you have to have pizzazz, you have to have style. Problem is, you cannot buy pizzazz in a supermarket (I tried once and came out with two frozen pizzas instead), but you can learn the tricks of great presentation.

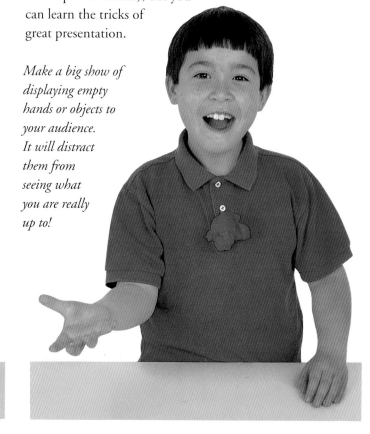

Make a big show of displaying empty hands or objects to your audience. It will distract them from seeing what you are really up to!

My last tip to you is this – let the audience know you have finished a trick by taking a small bow. Save the big bow until the end. As soon as they see you bow, the audience will clap and call out for more.

Entertaining style

This one is easy to explain. If you have a smile on your face and look as though you are enjoying what you are doing, the audience will also enjoy themselves. Try to look confident and relaxed. When you talk to your audience, speak clearly and loudly. No one will hear your great jokes if you mumble and mutter.

Professional style

If the audience ask you to repeat a trick or to tell them how it was done, refuse politely. If you tell all your secrets, you will have to learn a whole new routine, and a trick is never as good second time around.

This boy has magical style. He is smiling, wearing his favourite hat and looks ready to take a big bow.

Sometimes it helps to look as surprised as your audience.

Dress style

The traditional costume for a magician is a smart suit, bow tie and flashy cape. Nowadays almost any sort of costume is fine. A colourful waistcoat and a pair of jeans can look just as smart and professional. If you want to work out your own wacky costume, go ahead. My rule is – if you feel good, you will look good.

Stage style

To be a show-stopping performer, you must know the secrets of the trade. The first is, always enter from the side or from the back of the stage. Then walk to the middle, smile at your audience and wait for the applause.

The second thing to do is introduce yourself to the audience. You can use your own name or invent a colourful stage-name.

Number three is always to face your audience. This will mean that your props, or equipment, will have to be within easy reach. Your audience have not come to watch you rummage upside-down in a box.

The fourth trade secret is this – if you make a mistake or a trick does not work, try to laugh it off. You can even pretend that the mistake was meant to happen. Then you can do the trick again, but this time do it correctly.

Materials

These are some of the main materials and items of equipment you will need.

Carbon copy paper When placed between two sheets of paper, inky side down, it will copy whatever is written on the top sheet of paper.

Coloured and white paper and card For many of the projects, you can recycle pieces of paper and use card from cut-up cereal boxes. Large sheets of card can be bought in stationery shops and craft shops.

Marker pen A marker pen is a type of felt-tip pen that draws quite thick lines. If you do not have a marker pen, use an ordinary felt-tip pen instead.

Paperclips A good collection of paperclips is vital for any promising magician.

PVA glue This is a strong glue that can be used to stick together paper, wood or even fabric. It can bought in stationery shops and is sometimes called craft glue or white glue. You will need a brush or glue spreader to apply the glue.

Recycled boxes For the projects in this book, you will need two empty boxes – a large one and a small one. A cereal box and a small tea or chocolate box would be ideal.

Rubber bands These are almost as important to the budding magician as paperclips. You can buy bags of assorted rubber bands in stationery shops.

Ruler Accurate measuring is required for some projects so you will need a ruler divided into centimetres (cm) or inches (in).

Safety scissors Safety scissors are smaller than cutting scissors. Their edges are rounded and the blades are not as sharp as normal scissors.

Sticky-back plastic This plastic material comes in many colours and designs. It is usually bought in rolls. To make it adhere to a surface, you simply peel off the protective backing and press the sticky-back plastic on to the object.

String It does not matter if you use plain or coloured string as long as you have lots of it.

String

Rubber bands

Sticky tape

Recycled box

Sticky-back plastic

Coloured and white paper and card

Paperclips

Safety scissors

Paper bag

Electrical tape

PVA glue

Ruler

Marker pen

Carbon copy paper

Equipment

Lemon

Crunchy cereal

Skittle

Scarves

Coins

Sticky tack

Plastic squeakers

Hat

Large playing card

Pack of playing cards

Sweets in wrappers

Coins You can use real or plastic toy money when practising or performing tricks. You will need five coins.

Crunchy cereal Use a breakfast cereal made of large, crunchy flakes. Ask permission before raiding the kitchen!

Hat All magicians have got to have a hat – your audience will expect it! It can be a dashing top hat, a favourite baseball cap or even a crazy sunhat.

Large playing card This is about four times the size of a normal playing card. You can buy it in joke shops and toy shops.

Lemon You can use a real or plastic lemon to do the Magic Box trick.

Plastic squeakers These are round, plastic discs that squeak when squeezed. You can buy them in joke shops and toy shops. They are not expensive.

Playing cards A pack of playing cards consists of 52 cards plus two jokers. There are four suits – hearts, diamonds, clubs and spades – numbered from ace to king. There are two black suits and two red suits. To do all the tricks you will need two packs of cards. Playing cards are inexpensive and can be bought in toy shops and stationery shops.

Scarves You can use large or small silky scarves or handkerchieves. Brightly coloured or patterned ones are best.

Skittle This is used when playing indoor or garden bowls. It is made of plastic.

Sticky tack This reusable material is used to fix posters on to walls. You can buy it in packs in stationery shops.

Sweets in wrappers You will need quite a few sweets wrapped in foil or cellophane. Do not start eating them before you have completed the trick!

Missing Money

This trick is every magician's favourite. Why? Because it cannot go wrong. All you need are five coins and some sticky tape fixed to the palm of your hand. Keep the palm of your hand hidden throughout the trick, otherwise the audience will work out your secret.

Handy hint

In place of a loop of sticky tape you can use a small piece of double-sided tape. Use small coins rather than large ones – large coins are harder to conceal and too heavy to adhere to the tape. You can use plastic coins if you like.

YOU WILL NEED THESE MATERIALS

5 small coins of the same size

Strong, clear sticky tape

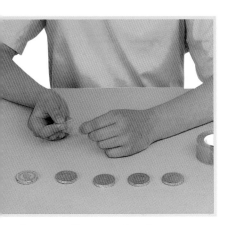

1 Cut a small piece of sticky tape about 5cm (2in) long. Overlap the ends, sticky side out, to make a loop. Place the five coins in front of you on the table.

2 Firmly press the loop of tape on to the palm of your hand. Do not let anyone see you doing this. This little bit of magical sneakiness is just between you and me.

3 Make a big show of counting the five coins one-by-one as you stack them neatly one on top of the other. Ask your audience to count along with you.

4 Press the hand with the sticky loop on to the pile of coins. Say your chosen magic words and then withdraw your hand. The top coin will be stuck to the loop.

5 Keep the palm concealing the coin flat on the table. With the other hand, spread out the pile of coins and count them out loud. Yikes! There are now only four coins.

It is a secret!

In this trick, the missing coin remains missing. You do not reveal where you have concealed the fifth coin. Remove the coin and sticky tape from your hand discreetly while you are returning the other coins to your pocket or to your magic box.

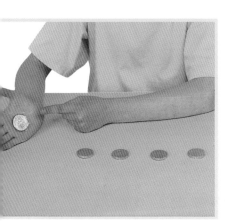

6 The fifth coin, of course, is still stuck to your hand.

Tricky Tubes

This is another classic trick that is used by magicians everywhere. It involves moving a handkerchief from one 'magic' tube to another tube to give the impression that both tubes are empty. In the finale of this trick you stun the audience by producing a handkerchief from the empty tubes.

YOU WILL NEED THESE MATERIALS

2 pieces of different coloured card 30cm x 30cm (12in x 12in)

Rubber band

Small handkerchief

9 paperclips

1 Steps 1, 2 and 3 show what you have to do to prepare for this trick. Roll the pieces of card to make tubes. One tube must be narrower so that it will fit inside the larger tube. Secure the tubes with eight paperclips.

2 The device that makes this trick work is a paperclip. Unfold the paperclip to make hooks at either end, as shown. Attach a rubber band to one hook. Roll up the handkerchief and thread it into the rubber band.

3 Hook the other end of the paperclip on to the top of the narrow tube. The rubber band and the handkerchief will be on the inside of the tube. Make sure that the handkerchief is totally hidden from view.

4 Now it is time to get this show on the road! Hold up the large tube so that the audience can see that it is completely empty. This should not be difficult as it really is empty!

5 Pick up the narrow tube and slide it slowly down through the large tube. As you do this the paperclip holding the handkerchief will hook itself on to the large tube.

6 Pull the narrow tube out from the bottom of the large tube. Then, with a flourish, hold up the narrow tube to show your audience that it is empty.

7 Place the narrow tube on the table. Slide the large tube over the narrow tube. The handkerchief will fall inside the narrow tube. Then say to your audience, 'From two empty tubes I will magically produce a handkerchief.' Pull the handkerchief from inside the narrow tube. All you have to do now is wait for the applause and take a bow!

Magic Box

The Magic Box can produce objects out of thin air. One minute the box is empty, the next it is not. Only you know about the secret box that can hold a lemon, a pack of cards or even an elephant. If you are going to pull an elephant out of the box, perhaps this trick should be called the Magic Trunk!

Practice makes perfect

To get this trick right takes lots of practice. You should be so familiar with it that the audience are not even aware that you turn the box around in step 8. One wrong move and the lemon (or the elephant) will come tumbling out for all the world to see! To make this trick really impressive, ask someone in the audience to lend you their watch, wallet or sunglasses. Their mouth will drop when they see their object disappear and then reappear.

YOU WILL NEED THESE MATERIALS

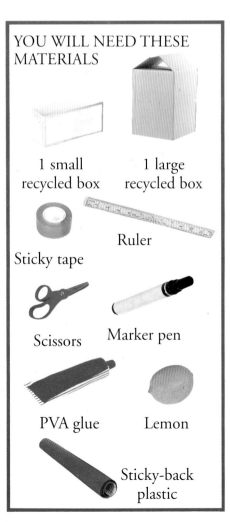

1 small recycled box

1 large recycled box

Sticky tape

Ruler

Scissors

Marker pen

PVA glue

Lemon

Sticky-back plastic

1 To make the Magic Box, tape the ends of the boxes closed. Cut the top off the small box. Use the marker pen and ruler to draw a line along one long and two short edges of the large box.

2 Cut along these lines carefully to make a hinged lid on the large box. By the way, did I tell you to empty the boxes before you started this project? Oops, oh well!

3 Do the same to the other side of the large box but this time the hinged lid is on the opposite edge. You must get this right or the Magic Box will not be very magical.

4 Tape, glue or nail the small box securely to the inside of one of the hinged lids. (Forget nailing – I was just joking.) The opened top of the small box must face where the lid is hinged.

5 Cover the box with sticky-back plastic. Cut two strips of plastic to make tabs. Fix tabs to the outside edge of the lids, fold in half and fix to the inside edge. Put the lemon in the small box.

6 Now it is magic time! Place the box on the table. The lid containing the small box is on the bottom with the tab nearest you. Hold on to both tabs because you are about to open the box.

7 Raise the box and pull on the tabs to open both lids. Say to your audience, "This box is empty – but not for long." Lay the box on the table.

8 The lid containing the lemon should be on the bottom. Turn the box around, hold the tab and lift the lid. Hold up the lemon to the audience.

79

The Big Picture

So that you can say hello or farewell to your audience in a magical way, I have prepared this special trick. It is a very simple illusion where a small picture suddenly becomes a big picture. Carefully follow the instructions for folding the paper, or you will be saying hello or goodbye to yourself.

YOU WILL NEED THESE MATERIALS

Marker pen

2 sheets of paper

PVA glue   Scissors

This is how the trick starts. You show the small picture, then, with a quick flick of your wrist, it suddenly becomes the Big Picture!

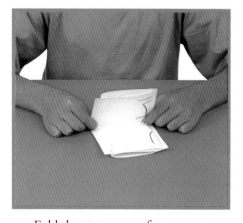

1 To prepare for this trick, place a sheet of paper with a long side nearest you. Draw a large picture of someone waving on the paper. Keep the drawing simple, you will have to repeat it later.

2 Turn the paper so that the picture is upside-down. Fold the paper concertina-style making the right hand flap larger than the other two. The right hand flap is on the bottom, as shown.

3 Fold the paper away from you, so that the top flap is a little smaller than the bottom flap. I know this sounds complicated, but it is easy. I could not do it if it was too hard.

4 Take the other sheet of paper and cut out a rectangle that is exactly the same size as the bottom flap of the folded paper. On to this rectangle, draw the picture that is on the folded paper.

5 Glue this picture on to the front of the large flap. The bottom of the picture will be nearest the fold. (See, I told you this is easy!) Apply the glue carefully so that it does not spread on to the other flaps. You are ready to present the Big Picture.

6 Hold the paper, as shown, with the fold at the bottom and the small drawing facing the audience. To stop the paper unfolding, support the flap with a little finger. Tell the audience that you are going to give them a cheery welcome or a sad farewell wave.

7 Quickly pull sideways so that the folded paper unfolds and the big picture is revealed.

Before their very eyes, the audience have seen the small picture become a great, big picture. If you have been an ace magician and practised this routine lots of times, then your audience will be totally taken in by the illusion. In place of a drawing you could write a message, like "Welcome to the Greatest Show on Earth!"

The Big Card Trick

You may have seen this trick performed many times, but now you will be able to do it yourself. You can choose any number or suit you want for the large playing card, but a card of the same number and suit must be at the top of your pack of playing cards. The two cards fixed to the large card must be numerically smaller than the big card.

Handy hint

You can make your own large playing card with stiff white card and a black marker pen. It does not matter which suit or number you choose to draw, as long as it is the same as the top card on your pack of cards.

YOU WILL NEED THESE MATERIALS

Pack of playing cards and 1 large envelope

Sticky tack

Large playing card

1 To prepare for this trick, use a small piece of sticky tack to fix a two and four of any suit on to the back of the large ten of clubs card. Place them in the envelope. Also check that the ten of clubs is the top card on your pack of playing cards. Now let the show begin.

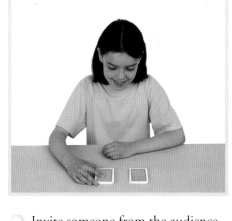

2 Invite someone from the audience to join you on stage and cut the pack of cards. No, not with a pair of scissors. To cut the cards, all your guest has to do is take a pile of cards off the top of the pack and lay them beside the remaining cards.

3 Place the bottom half of the pack on top of the other cards. Place it so that it is at right angles to the cut cards. This will show you where the pack was cut and where you will find the ten of clubs. Tell your guest that they will shortly see their secret card.

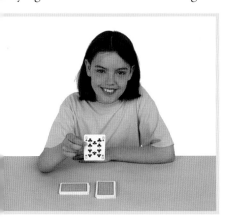

4 Remove the upper stack of cards from the pile and turn over the next card. Without looking at the card, show it to your guest. Tell them that they must remember what their secret card is. You know that it is the ten of clubs!

5 Ask your guest to shuffle the cards as much as they like. When they are shuffled, you can put them into the envelope. This envelope contains the large ten of clubs card plus the two other smaller cards.

6 Tell your guest that you are going to find their secret card. Put your hand into the envelope and pull out the two card. Ask if this is the secret card. They will say no. You then ask, 'Is it bigger than this?'

7 Repeat the routine as in step 6, but this time pull out the four card. It is now your big moment to astound and amuse everyone. Put your hand into the envelope again and pull out the large ten of clubs card. Show it to your guest and say, 'Is this big enough?' You have shown your guest that you knew that their chosen card was the ten of clubs all the time.

See the Unseen

Here are two techniques for seeing the unseen – reading messages that you were never intended to read. For the first method you have to get hold of the notepad quickly.

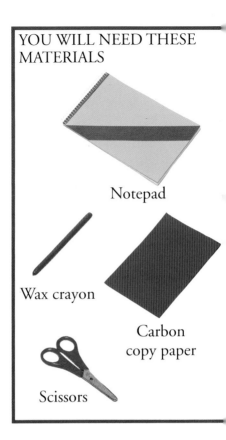

Notepad

Wax crayon

Carbon copy paper

Scissors

1 **Method 1** – Get the notepad on which the torn-out message was written. Rub the crayon gently over the top sheet. The impressions made by the written message will remain unshaded.

2 **Method 2** – To intercept a message, trim a sheet of carbon copy paper so that it is smaller than the notepad. Turn over two pages of the notepad and insert the copy paper inky side down.

3 Once the message has been written and the person is out of sight, turn the top pages of the notepad over and remove the copy paper. On the page below will be a copy of the message. Take care doing this and never attempt to intercept truly personal messages.

Noisy Alarms

Crunch, crackle, pop, squeak! What are those noises? They are the sounds of your bedroom security devices going noisily into action. I bet the intruder got a surprise!

YOU WILL NEED THESE MATERIALS

Crunchy cereal   2 plastic squeakers

Handy hint

You will have to keep changing the positions of your alarms or they will prove ineffective against intruders.

1 **Noisy warning 1** – This may sound a little odd, but crunchy cereal makes a great night-time alarm. All you have to do is leave a pile of cereal just outside your bedroom door.

2 When the unwitting intruder steps on the cereal, you will hear the crunch, crackle and pop! The intruder will realize that their sneaky game is up and will run away.

3 **Noisy warning 2** – In case the intruder misses the crunchy cereal alarm, place one plastic squeaker under a rug near the door and another under the cushion of a chair. (Even intruders have to sit down sometime!) Now all you have to do is wait.

When you hear the squeakers 'squeak' you will know that you have not caught a mouse, but a sneaky rat!

Trick Wallet

Open one flap of this wallet and it is empty. Open it the other way and – wow! – there is the secret document. Make two identical Trick Wallets so that you and a friend can switch wallets (and secret information) without being detected. When using the wallet to play a trick on someone, distract his or her attention so that they do not notice you turning the wallet over.

Handy hint

If you are going to use your Trick Wallet as part of a magic act, the wallet should be quite large. This will make it easier for the audience to see what is and what is not happening. When using the wallet for secret messages, make sure it will fit easily into a pocket.

YOU WILL NEED THESE MATERIALS

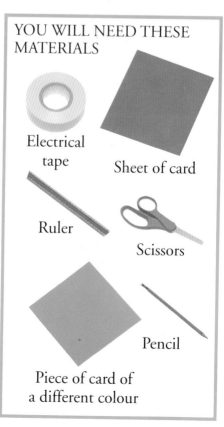

Electrical tape

Sheet of card

Ruler

Scissors

Pencil

Piece of card of a different colour

1 Measure and draw three rectangles, each 20cm x 8cm (8in x 3in) on to the sheet of card. Cut out the rectangles. You can make a big wallet by cutting out three larger rectangles.

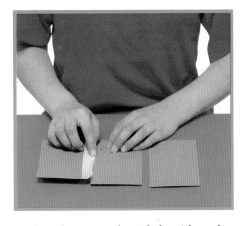

2 Lay the rectangles side by side and join the edges with electrical tape, as shown. The tape should act like a hinge, allowing each piece of card to fold over easily.

3 Tape the joins on the back of the card and fix electrical tape along the remaining two short sides. Position the tape so that it can be folded over to the back to give a neat finish.

4 Concertina-fold the wallet, as shown. Lay the wallet on to the table and gently press it flat.

5 To test the Trick Wallet, place a small rectangle of the other coloured card between two of the flaps. Close the flaps. Turn the wallet over and open the flap. If the flap is empty you are doing the right thing. Close this flap.

Magic trick wallet

To make the wallet work in a magic show routine, you have to be discreet when turning the wallet over so that your audience does not catch on to the trick. The only way to achieve this sleight of hand is to distract them by making a funny face or telling a joke. A good magician always has (among other things!) a couple of good jokes up his or her sleeve.

6 Turn the wallet over again and open the flap. If all has gone to plan, the flap will contain the piece of card.

Joke in the Post

Want to send someone a shocking surprise? All it takes is paper, paperclips and sticky tape. Joke in the Post is so easy to assemble that you could make one for each of your friends. But will they still be your friends after you have played this joke on them?

1 Fold the sheet of paper or thin card into equal thirds. Press the folds flat with your hands and then open out the paper again.

2 Open out two paperclips to make L-shapes, as shown. Bend and shape another paperclip to form a circle. Do this carefully – the ends are sharp.

3 Tape the L-shape paperclips to the paper and loop rubber bands around the ends, as shown. Thread the rubber bands on to the wire circle.

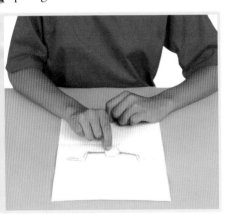

4 Slowly wind the wire circle around and around. The rubber bands will twist and tighten. Whatever you do, do not let go!

5 Re-fold the paper without letting go of the wire circle. Carefully insert the folded paper into the envelope and seal it.

6 Address the envelope using the marker pen. Post or deliver the envelope to your friend.

7 When your friend opens the letter the rubber bands will unwind causing the wire circle to spin and clatter against the paper. This is bound to make your friend jump in fright.

Handy Signals

Getting messages to friends can be tricky when you are involved in a hush-hush surveillance operation or you are working in the library. So instead of shouting messages, use hand signals. On the next page are examples of just a handful (ha, ha!) of hand signals and their meanings. Use them alone to convey a simple message or link them together for more complicated instructions. When you have mastered these signals, go on to invent your own.

YOU WILL NEED

Your hands (preferably still attached to your body!)

1 Quiet! – Press a finger to your lips when you want someone to stop talking. Move the finger over to your ear to say 'listen.'

2 Yes and no – Resting your chin on a hand with the thumb pointing up means 'yes.' To say 'no', point the thumb down.

3 Danger warning – Place a hand loosely around your throat to warn friends that the situation is dangerous and to take care.

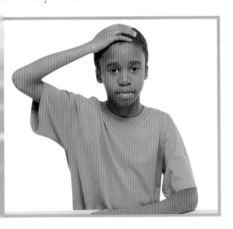

4 Come here – Running a hand through your hair from the front to the back means 'come here.'

5 Go away – Hiding your face behind one hand means 'go away'. Use two hands to say 'go away quickly.'

6 Look – Placing a finger next to the right eye means 'look right.' A finger next to the left eye means 'look left.' Fingers next to both eyes means look straight ahead.

When you have mastered these signals, go on to invent your own. But before you forget what each new signal means, write it down.

Final Challenge

Your mission is to rescue the skittle from the circle using only string and a rubber band. You and your accomplice cannot enter the circle, nor touch the skittle. The only bit of floor the skittle can touch is the area on which it is standing. Good luck!

YOU WILL NEED THESE MATERIALS

Scissors

Rubber band

Balls of string

Plastic skittle

The Final Challenge is not easy, but that makes it all the more challenging. Now it is time to put your thinking caps on – there is a poor damsel skittle in distress that needs to be rescued.

1 Draw a circle 1¹/₂m (48in) in diameter using the chalk. (A hoop is used here for clarity). Place the skittle in the middle of the circle. Cut four lengths of string 2m (2yd) long.

2 Thread lengths of string through the rubber band. The rubber band should be midway along each string. Hold the ends of the strings, as shown.

3 Gently pull on the strings to stretch the rubber band so that it will fit easily over the top of the skittle. Lower the rubber band over the neck of the skittle.

4 Allow the rubber band to tighten around the skittle by relaxing your pull on the strings. Carefully raise the skittle out of the circle. Do not pull on the strings as this will loosen the rubber band's grip on the skittle.

5 Congratulations, you have done it! Now see if your friends can do it.

This is a great game to play at a party. To make it more difficult for your friends, you can set a time limit in which the challenge must be completed.

Index

A

Appearing bubble 63

B

Back-flip card 28-29
Balloon balls 44
Balloon house 66-67
Balloon modelling 40, 41, 42-43
   balloon house 66-67
   big elephant 58
   birthday cards 43
   bunch of tulips 64
   dashing sword 61
   decorating balloons 41, 43
   inflating balloons 41, 42, 43
   king of hearts 60
   knotting balloons 42
   pampered pooch 56
   parrot on a perch 57
   safety 43
   sunflowers 65
   tiny mouse 59
Balloon pumps 41
Balloon tricks 42, 43, 62-63
Bananas, juggling 53
Bean bags 41, 45

Behind the back throw 47
Big card trick 82-83
Big elephant 58
Big picture 80-81
Birthday cards, balloon 43
Black paint 13
Boxes, magic 9, 78-79
   time-bomb escape 36-37
Bunch of tulips 64

C

Cards 12, 73
   back-flip card 28-29
   big card trick 82-83
   shuffling 12
Cereal alarm 85
Chocolate coins 16
Clap in time exercise 47
Coins 12, 73
   coin fold 20-21
   coin through hand 30-31
   cutting 22-23
   missing money 74-75
   money from nowhere 16-17
Costume 10, 71
Crazy juggling 52
Cups and balls 24-25
Cutting coins 22-23

D

Dashing sword 61
Dirty napkin trick 14-15
Dizzy spin throw 47
Dog balloon model 56

E

Effects 12
Egg in a box 9
Elephant balloon model 58
Envelopes
   big card trick 82-83

postman's wand 26-27
Equipment and materials 12-13, 41, 72-73
Escape trick 36-37
eyes, using your 11, 22-23

F

Fakes 12
Felt-tip pens 41, 43
Final challenge 92-93
Flowers, balloon 64-65

G

Gags 12
Gimmicks 12
Greetings cards, balloon 43

H

Hand, coin through 30-31
Handkerchiefs and scarves 12, 73
   in a box 9
   in a hat 10
   juggling with 50
   purple hanky, red hanky 32-33
   tricky tubes 76-77
Handy signals 90-91
Hard workout 47
Hats 10, 73
   king of hearts model 60
   making 10
   middle house mouse 24-25
   money from nowhere 16-17
Houdini 36
House, balloon 66-67

...lusions 9, 12, 80-81
...npromptu tricks 30
...flating balloons 41, 42, 43

...oke in the post 88-89
...okes 11, 12, 71, 87
...uggler's nightmare 48, 49
...ggling 40
balls 41, 44
bean bags 41, 45
behind the back throw 47
clap in time exercise 47
clubs 41, 55
crazy juggling 52
dizzy spin throw 47
hard workout 47
juggler's nightmare 48, 49
monkey juggling 53
one-ball workout 46-47
over the shoulder juggle 55
rings 41
safety 43
three-ball frenzy 50-51
two-ball juggle 48-49
under the leg throw 47

K

King of hearts 60
Knotting balloons 42

L

Left-handedness 13, 54
Letters, joke in the post 88-89
Loads 12

M

Magic balloon 63
Magic boxes 9, 78-79
Magic wands see Wands
Magnetic wand 18-19
Materials 13, 41, 72
Mice
balloon model 59
middle house 24-25
Middle house mouse 24-25
Misdirection 11, 20-21, 22-23
Missing money 74-75
Mistakes, dealing with 11
Money
missing 74-75
money from nowhere 16-17
see also Coins
Monkey juggling 53

N

Napkin trick 14-15
Noisy alarms 85

O

One-ball workout 46-47
Over the shoulder juggle 55

P

Painless wand 19
Palming 12
Pampered pooch 56
Parrot on a perch 57
Patter 11, 12
Performing techniques 11-12, 70-71
Postman's wand 26-27
Preparation 63, 70
Presentation 11-12, 70-71

Production 12
Props 8-13
Purple hanky, red hanky 32-33

R

Rabbit in a box 9
radio magic box 9
Repeating tricks 11, 71
Ringing up 34-35
Routine 12

S

Safety tips 43
Scarves see Handkerchiefs and scarves
Secrets 11, 71
See the unseen 84
Sewing bean bags 45-46
Shuffle 12
Signals 90-91
Silks 12, 73
Sleeving 12
cutting coins 22-23
Sleight of hand 12
Squeaker alarm 85
Stealing 13
Stickers 41, 43
Sunflowers 65
Switching 13
Sword balloon model 61
Squeaker alarm 85

Stealing 13
Sunflowers 65
Switching 13
Sword balloon model 61

T

Talk 13
Three-ball frenzy 50-51
Time-bomb escape 36-37
Tiny mouse 59
Transposition 13
Trick wallet 86-87
Tricky tubes 76-77
Two-ball juggle 48-49

U

Under the leg throw 47
Under or over 54-55

V

Vanishing 13

W

Wallet, trick 86-87
Wands
   magic 8, 18-19
   magnetic 18-19
   making 8
   painless 19
   postman's wand 26-27
   ringing up 34-35
wobbly 19
Wobbly wand 19
Words, magic 12-13

X

X-ray wand 34-35

Acknowledgements

The publishers would like to thank the following children for appearing in this book, and of course their parents
Nana Addae, Richard Addae, Michelle Apeagyei, Steve Jason Aristizabal, Joshua Ashford, Rula Awad,
Nadia el-Ayadi, Nicola Barnard, Michael Bewley, Emma Blue, Leah Bone, Cerys Brunsdon, William Carabine,
Alexander Clare, Emma Cotton, Charli Coulson, Laurence Defraitus, Alaba Fashina, Fiona Fulton,
Nicola Game, Lana Green, Laura Harris-Stewart, Jonathan Headon, Gerald Ishiekwene, Stella-Rae James,
Aribibia Johnson, Reece Johnson, Carl Keating, Camille Kenny-Ryder, Lee Knight, Kevin Lake, Barry Lee,
Kirsty Lee, Isaac John Lewis, Alex Lindblom-Smith, Scott Longstaff, Laura Masters, Claire McCarthy,
Erin McCarthy, Trevor Meechan, Hugh Hong Mo, Jessica Moxley, Lucy Nightingale, Ify Obi, Adenike Odeleye,
Wura Odurinde, Laurence Ody, Abayomi Ojo, Fola Oladimeji, Ola Olawe, Michael Oloyede, Yemisi Omolewa,
Tope Oni, Josephina Quayson, Pedro Henrique Queiroz, Jamie Rosso,
Nida Sayeed, Charlie Simpson, Justine Spiers, Nicola Twiner, Sarah Twiner,
Frankie David Viner, Nhat Han Vong, Devika Webb, Tanel Yusef.

Contributors: Petra Boase, Stephanie Donaldson, Nick Huckleberry Beak,
Sarah Maxwell, Hugh Nightingale, Steve and Jane Parker, Michael Purton,
Thomasina Smith, Jacki Wadeson, Sally Walton. Gratitude also to
Hampden Gurney School, Walnut Tree Walk Primary School and
St John the Baptist Church of England School.

The authors would like to thank the following for their assistance in
providing materials and advice:

Boots; Dylon Consumer Advice; Head Gardener, Knightsbridge; Lady
Jayne; Mason Pearson, Kent; Molton Brown; Tesco. Special thanks to
Justin of Air Circus; 'Smiley Face' from Theatre Crew, Tunbridge Wells;
and the Bristol Juggling Convention.